WORD PROBLEMS WITH WOLVES

By Rory McDonnell

leveled reader
math

Please visit our website, www.garethstevens.com. For a free color catalog of all our high-quality books, call toll free 1-800-542-2595 or fax 1-877-542-2596.

Cataloging-in-Publication Data

Names: McDonnell, Rory.
Title: Word problems with wolves / Rory McDonnell.
Description: New York : Gareth Stevens Publishing, 2018. | Series: Animal math | Includes index.
Identifiers: ISBN 9781538208687 (pbk.) | ISBN 9781538208700 (library bound) | ISBN 9781538208694 (6 pack)
Subjects: LCSH: Word problems (Mathematics)–Juvenile literature. | Problem solving–Juvenile literature. | Wolves–Juvenile literature.
Classification: LCC QA63.M35545 2018 | DDC 513.2–dc23

Published in 2018 by
Gareth Stevens Publishing
111 East 14th Street, Suite 349
New York, NY 10003

Copyright © 2018 Gareth Stevens Publishing

Designer: Sarah Liddell
Editor: Therese Shea

Photo credits: Cover, p. 1 David Dirga/Shutterstock.com; background used throughout T. Sumaetho/Shutterstock.com; p. 5 Scenic Shutterbug/Shutterstock.com; p. 7 (gray wolf) miroslav chytil/Shutterstock.com; p. 7 (red wolf) Jean-Edouard Rozey/Shutterstock.com; p. 7 (Ethiopian wolf) Alberto Loyo/Shutterstock.com; p. 9 Dennis W Donohue/Shutterstock.com; p. 11 Through Christy's Lens/Shutterstock.com; p. 13 Michael Roeder/Shutterstock.com; p. 15 Tom Reichner/Shutterstock.com; pp. 17, 21 Bildagentur Zoonar GmbH/Shutterstock.com; p. 19 Jim Cumming/Shutterstock.com.

Printed in China

CPSIA compliance information: Batch #CW18GS: For further information contact Gareth Stevens, New York, New York at 1-800-542-2595.

Contents

Boldface words appear in the glossary.

Wolves and Word Problems

Wolves are in the dog family. They're known for being brave and smart. Wolves can help us **solve** word problems! Check your answers on page 22.

A park ranger sees 9 wolves. Then, 2 wolves run away. How many wolves are left?

Wolf Species

There are 3 species, or kinds, of wolves. They are gray wolves, red wolves, and Ethiopian wolves.

There are 2 gray wolves, 1 red wolf, and 1 Ethiopian wolf. How many wolves are there in all?

gray wolf

red wolf

Ethiopian wolf

7

Most wolves in North America are gray wolves. Gray wolves are sometimes called timber wolves. Their fur can be gray, brown, red, white, or black.

Two wolves have brown fur. Three wolves have gray fur. One wolf has white fur. How many wolves are there in all?

Join the Pack!

Wolves live in groups called packs. A male wolf and female wolf lead the pack. They're called the alpha male and alpha female.

A pack has 5 wolves. More wolves join. There are now 10 wolves in the pack. How many wolves joined the pack?

Wolf packs are often made up of 4 to 9 wolves. Some packs are as large as 30 wolves! Packs this large may break up into smaller packs.

There's a pack of 20 wolves. Then, 10 wolves leave. How many wolves are left?

Wolf packs hunt at night. They eat animals such as deer, moose, sheep, squirrels, rabbits, birds, snakes, and mice.

A wolf pack catches 3 deer. First, 1 deer runs away. Then, 1 more runs away. How many deer are left?

15

Wolves can run fast. They walk a lot each day. Sometimes the pack gets separated. They **howl** to find each other!

There are 11 wolves in a pack. They meet a pack of 15 wolves. How many wolves are there in all?

16

Wolf Talk

Wolves **communicate**! They bark to warn of danger. When they want to play, they dance or bow.

There are wolves in the woods. Then, 4 more wolves join them. There are now 14 wolves in the woods. How many were there to start?

Wolf Pups!

The alpha male and alpha female have babies called pups. When the pups grow up, they join the pack, too!

There are 4 pups. First, 2 pups run away. Then, 1 pup comes back. How many pups are there now?

Glossary

communicate: to share thoughts or feelings by speaking, writing, moving, or acting in a certain way

howl: to make a long, loud cry that sounds sad

solve: to find the answer

Answer Key

page 4: 7 wolves

page 6: 4 wolves

page 8: 6 wolves

page 10: 5 wolves

page 12: 10 wolves

page 14: 1 deer

page 16: 26 wolves

page 18: 10 wolves

page 20: 3 pups

For More Information

Books

Johnson, Jinny. *Gray Wolf*. Mankato, MN: Smart Apple Media, 2014.

Pfeffer, Wendy. *Wolf Pup*. New York, NY: Sterling, 2011.

Somervill, Barbara A. *Gray Wolf*. Ann Arbor, MI: Cherry Lake Publishing, 2008.

Websites

Fun Wolf Facts
www.wolf.org/wolf-info/wild-kids/fun-facts/
Read some interesting numbers about wolves.

Gray Wolf
kids.nationalgeographic.com/animals/gray-wolf/
See a map of where these amazing animals live.

Index